Birth Control and Protection

Options for Teens

By Judith Peacock

Consultant:
Jennifer A. Oliphant, MPH
Research Fellow and Community Outreach Coordinator
National Teen Pregnancy Prevention Research Center
Division of General Pediatrics and Adolescent Health
University of Minnesota

Perspectives on Healthy Sexuality

LifeMatters
an imprint of Capstone Press
Mankato, Minnesota

LifeMatters books are published by Capstone Press
PO Box 669 • 151 Good Counsel Drive • Mankato, Minnesota 56002
http://www.capstone-press.com

Printed in the United States of America

Library of Congress Cataloging-in-Publication Data
Peacock, Judith, 1942–
      Birth control and protection: options for teens / by Judith Peacock.
          p.   cm.—(Perspectives on healthy sexuality)
      Includes bibliographical references and index.
      Summary: Explains reasons for using birth control (including abstinence) to prevent pregnancy and disease; provides options for making a decision and getting help; and describes available choices.
      ISBN 0-7368-0715-2 (book)
      1. Birth control—Juvenile literature. 2. Contraceptives—Juvenile literature. 3. Teenagers—Sexual behavior—Juvenile literature. 4. Sex instruction for teenagers—Juvenile literature. [1. Birth control. 2. Youth—Sexual behavior.] I. Title. II. Series.
      HQ766.8 .P43 2000
      363.9´6—dc21   00-025304
                                                CIP

Staff Credits
Rebecca Aldridge, editor; Adam Lazar, designer; Kim Danger, photo researcher

Photo Credits
Cover: PhotoDisc/©Barbara Penoyar
Index Stock Imagery/©Peter Ardito, 15; Craig Witkowski, 23; SW Production, 54
International Stock/©Michael Agliolo, 12
PhotoDisc/©Barbara Penoyar, 35
Photo Network/©Eric R. Berndt, 6; ©Agricola, 9; ©Esbin-Anderson, 59
©Stockbyte, 24
Uniphoto/©Llewellyn, 21, 31, 51; ©Jackson Smith, 40; ©Bob Daemmrich, 48
Visuals Unlimited/©Stan Flegler, 29; ©Science VU-IWHC, 38

Table of Contents

Chapter Overview

Birth control prevents or reduces the chance of getting pregnant. Protection reduces the chance of getting or spreading sexually transmitted diseases.

Birth control may be especially important for unmarried teens. Having a baby poses risks for teen parents, their children, and society.

Teens in the United States have higher rates of pregnancies and sexually transmitted diseases than teens in any other developed country. Some reasons may include poor sex education and lack of access to or fear of using birth control.

Teens need to make decisions about birth control and protection before they find themselves in risky situations. Being responsible about birth control and protection helps to ensure a healthy and happy future.

Chapter 1

Why Use Birth Control and Protection?

Making responsible decisions about sexual behavior helps to protect your health and safety. Teens involved in male-female relationships need to be concerned about birth control. All teens, whether in male-female, male-male, or female-female relationships, need to think about protection.

The Risks of Teen Pregnancy and Childbearing

Each year in the United States, almost 1 million teen girls become pregnant. Having a baby can be one of life's most wonderful experiences—if you are ready for it. Most teens are not ready to be parents. Teen pregnancy and childbearing often pose difficulties for the parents, the child, and society.

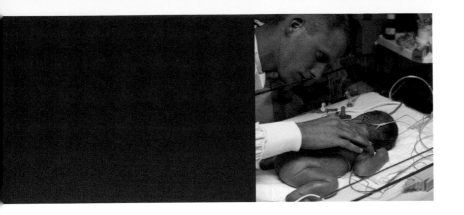

Teen Parents

Pregnancy and childbearing can damage a teen's physical health. This is especially true for girls younger than 15. Their body may not be fully developed and ready for childbirth. Teen girls have a higher rate of complications during pregnancy. They are more likely than adult women to have a long and difficult delivery.

Eighty percent of teen fathers do not marry the teen mother of their children. Some girls turn to their family for help with raising their child. However, raising a child takes a lot of time, energy, and money. Teen mothers may have difficulty finishing high school and finding a well-paying job.

Pregnancy and childbearing can be difficult for teens. It can cause feelings of stress, worry, and sadness. Most teens are not prepared emotionally to raise a child. They may become tired and impatient. They may resent having to care for a child while other teens are having fun.

The Child

Children born to teen mothers may have difficulty. Teens often do not seek medical care while pregnant. As a result, they are twice as likely as older women to have premature babies. These babies who are born too early are at risk for health problems. Teen girls can be loving mothers. However, many lack the knowledge and skills to provide the proper care a child needs.

Birth Control and Protection

According to the American Academy of Pediatrics (AAP), the media also contribute to the high rates of pregnancy and STDs among American teens. Television, movies, music, advertising, and the Internet contain countless references to sex. At the same time, there are few references to abstinence, condoms, or other forms of birth control and protection. The risks of unprotected sex seldom are mentioned. Teens may get the idea that everyone is sexually active and no one worries about pregnancy or STDs.

Society

Teen pregnancy and childbearing are costly to society. Teens who give birth and are from low-income families may not be able to pay for medical care. Many teen mothers need ongoing help with child care and other social services. Having a baby at a young age can keep teens living in poverty.

The Risks of Sexually Transmitted Diseases

People who become sexually active at a young age are likely to have several partners in their lifetime. The more partners a person has, the greater the chances of getting a sexually transmitted disease (STD). These also are called sexually transmitted infections (STIs). Certain condoms and continuous abstinence are the only forms of birth control that protect against STDs.

Teens with an STD may appear symptom-free. Symptoms of some STDs can take weeks, months, or years to appear. An infected teen may pass the disease on to a sexual partner and not know it.

STDs can have serious effects. STDs can lead to cancer and other chronic, or lifelong, illnesses. Some STDs, such as HIV, even may lead to death.

Sexually active teens give many reasons for not using birth control and protection. Here are a few:

"I didn't want my mother to find condoms in my drawer or pants pocket. Then she'd know I was having sex."
—Noah, age 16

"If I used birth control, that would mean I planned to have sex. Girls who plan to have sex are sluts."—Chrissi, age 15

"I feel funny asking my boyfriend to put on a condom. I don't want him to think I don't trust him."—Chua, age 17

Lana noticed a blister near her vagina. **Lana, Age 16** She ignored it, even though it hurt a lot. Later, Lana felt a burning pain down her legs and had flu-like symptoms. Lana's mom took Lana to the doctor. The doctor told Lana she had genital herpes. She could be bothered by symptoms for the rest of her life. Lana felt devastated. She knew her ex-boyfriend, Mike, had infected her. Lana trusted him when he said he was "clean." Why hadn't she insisted Mike use a condom anyway?

Teens and Birth Control and Protection

More than one-third of teens do not use birth control or protection during their first sexual experience. Many do not use birth control for up to a year after their first sexual experience.

Teens in the United States have more pregnancies than in any other developed country. The teen pregnancy rate in the United States is twice as high as the rate in England or Canada. It is nine times higher than the rate in the Netherlands or Japan.

Each year in the United States, approximately 3 million teens—or one in 4 sexually experienced teens—get an STD. About 3,000 teens have been diagnosed with AIDS. Use of protection can prevent these numbers from growing.

Why Teens Don't Use Birth Control and Protection

Teens in the United States are not more sexually active than teens in other countries. Then why are rates for unplanned pregnancy and STDs so high in the United States? Experts suggest several reasons.

One reason may be education. Compared with teens in other countries, many American teens do not receive clear and complete sex education. Younger teens especially tend to have false ideas about how pregnancy occurs and how it's prevented. Another reason may be a lack of access to free or low-cost reproductive health care. Finally, teens may encounter an attitude of secrecy and shame about birth control and protection.

Most teen pregnancies are not planned, but some teens want to get pregnant. They may see a baby as a way to keep a relationship. They may want something of their own to love. However, pregnancy is no guarantee of a lasting relationship, and babies cannot provide all the emotional support adults need.

Points to Consider

In your opinion, why don't some teens use birth control?

What is the attitude toward teen pregnancy among your friends and classmates? What is their attitude toward STDs?

Should the high rate of teen pregnancy and STDs in the United States concern people? Why?

Chapter Overview

There are many birth control methods. They include behavioral, barrier, and hormonal methods.

There are fewer methods of protection. They include some types of abstinence and condoms, dental dams, and possibly spermicides.

Birth control methods vary in effectiveness. They also vary in how easy they are to obtain and use. Teens should weigh the pros and cons of each method before making a choice.

In choosing birth control, teens must consider their level of sexual activity, lifestyle or life situation, and medical history. They also must consider their moral and religious values as well as their own personality.

To be effective, any birth control and protection method must be used correctly. It also must be used with every act of sexual intercourse.

Chapter 2

Birth Control and Protection Choices

How Pregnancy Happens

Knowing how pregnancy happens can help in understanding how birth control methods work. It also helps to know some of the main parts of the male and female reproductive systems. Here the female system is discussed more thoroughly than the male's system. This is because most birth control is based on the female body. Here's a review.

The Beginning of a Pregnancy

The union of a male sex cell (sperm) and a female sex cell (egg) is called fertilization. Pregnancy happens when a fertilized egg attaches itself to the lining of the uterus. After fertilization, it takes a few days following vaginal intercourse for pregnancy to occur.

The Male Sex Organ

The penis is the male sex organ. It usually is small and soft and hangs down. During sexual excitement, extra blood flows into the penis. It becomes larger and harder and stands away from the body. This is called an erection. During vaginal intercourse, the erect penis fits inside the female's vagina. It ejaculates, or squirts, semen into the vagina near the cervix. The sperm in this fluid start moving toward the female's uterus and fallopian tubes.

The Female Reproductive System

Ovaries. The ovaries are glands that contain hundreds of thousands of eggs. Females have two ovaries. About once a month beginning at puberty, an egg cell matures and is released. This process is called ovulation. Female hormones control it. A hormone is a chemical in the body that controls growth and sexual development. If the egg has not been fertilized, it dissolves. It passes out of the vagina along with blood and the contents of the lining of the uterus. This is called menstruation, or having a period.

Fallopian tubes. These tubes form the upper end of the uterus. The fringed end of the nearest tube draws the egg into the tube. Then the egg moves toward the uterus. The fallopian tube is where fertilization occurs.

Birth Control and Protection

Did You Know?

The semen deposited inside a female's vagina during sexual intercourse contains hundreds of millions of sperm cells.

Uterus. The uterus, or womb, is a hollow organ. The egg passes from the fallopian tube into the uterus. If the egg has been fertilized, it attaches to the wall of the uterus and grows into a baby.

Cervix. The cervix is a narrow passageway that connects the uterus and vagina. It allows blood to pass through during menstruation or semen to pass through during sex.

Vagina. The vagina is the tube that connects the cervix to the outside of the body.

Methods of Birth Control

Another name for the union of sperm and egg is conception. Birth control is *contra*ception, or "against" conception. Its purpose is to keep an egg from being fertilized and planting itself in the uterus. A device used to prevent pregnancy is called a contraceptive.

Birth control methods can be grouped according to how they work. Here are six main ways:

Behavioral methods. These depend on individuals or couples controlling their sexual behavior in certain ways. They include continuous abstinence, periodic abstinence, outercourse, and withdrawal.

Barrier methods. These devices block the sperm from joining the egg. They include male and female condoms, spermicides, diaphragms, and cervical caps.

Myth: People don't have to worry about HIV/AIDS anymore because new drugs can cure it.

Fact: Some new drugs do help people who have HIV/AIDS live better and longer. However, these drugs are only treatments, not cures. And some of the new treatments do not work for many people.

Hormonal methods. These use synthetic hormones made in a laboratory. They alter a female's reproductive cycle. Some prevent an egg from being released by the ovaries. Others prevent an egg from attaching to the wall of the uterus. Hormonal methods include birth control pills, shots, and implants.

Intrauterine device (IUD). This device is made of plastic and copper. An IUD is put in the uterus to prevent sperm from meeting an egg. A teen's uterus usually is too small to hold an IUD in place.

Emergency contraception. This special mix of birth control pills or IUD prevents pregnancy after unprotected sex.

Nonreversible methods. These methods prevent pregnancy on a permanent basis. They include cutting the male's sperm duct (a vasectomy) or cutting or blocking the female's fallopian tubes (tubal ligation). These methods are not recommended for teens because of their permanence.

Choosing Birth Control

Teens need to choose the birth control method that is right for them. Choosing a method just because a friend uses it is not a good idea. The following factors influence a person's choice. Their level of importance is different for everyone.

Level of sexual activity. Some birth control methods provide ongoing protection against pregnancy. Others are used only on an as-needed basis. How often people have sex may determine their choice.

Lifestyle or life situation. The ability to pay for birth control may be a factor. The ease with which birth control can be obtained and used may be a factor, too. People may lack access to a health clinic that provides help with birth control.

Medical history. Past illnesses or medical conditions may prevent some people from using certain birth control.

Moral and religious values. Personal beliefs about birth control may limit choices.

Personality. Traits such as being shy or impatient may influence birth control choice. For example, birth control pills must be taken every day. This method may not be suitable for someone who is forgetful.

Effectiveness against STDs. Protection against STDs is important because teens are not likely to be in long-term, committed relationships.

How STDs Are Spread

STDs can be spread through sexual contact with someone who is infected. Bacteria, viruses, and other organisms cause STDs.

STDs caused by bacteria can be cured with antibiotics if discovered and treated soon enough. Otherwise, serious health problems can occur. STDs caused by viruses last throughout a person's life. They are treatable but not curable. Some of these STDs can lead to serious health problems and even death. Parasites, or organisms that live on or in another living being, cause some STDs. These STDs can be treated.

Methods of Protection

Continuous abstinence is the only sure way to prevent the spread of STDs. Protected sex is safer sex. That means there is less likelihood of spreading disease, but transmission still can occur. Chapters 3 and 4 discuss the different types of protection.

Responsible Use of Birth Control and Protection

"You're seven weeks pregnant, Faith." **Faith, Age 16** Faith stared at the doctor. How could she be pregnant? She and her boyfriend, Kenny, usually used birth control. Then Faith remembered. They both had gotten high a while back and didn't bother to use a condom.

Teens sometimes have false ideas about birth control. The following methods do not prevent pregnancy:

Having sex during the girl's period

Squirting water, douche, a soft drink, or vinegar into the vagina after intercourse; forcing liquid into the vagina is called douching. In fact, an additional stream of fluid may aid sperm in their journey.

Jumping up and down after intercourse

Having sex standing up or having the female on top of the male

Going to the bathroom right after intercourse: However, this is a good way to help prevent some infections in females.

To be effective, birth control and protection must be used every time a teen has sex. They also must be used correctly. Both partners should be involved. They should talk about birth control and protection before sexual activity. They also should choose a method satisfactory to both. Responsible use of birth control and protection requires determination and hard work. However, using a method consistently can decrease worry about pregnancy and STDs and increase sexual pleasure.

Points to Consider

If a teen boy and girl are dating and using birth control, are they protected against STDs? Why or why not?

Do you think birth control is seen equally as a man and woman's responsibility? Explain.

Who are people you could go to for advice on birth control and protection? Why would you choose these people?

Chapter Overview

The different forms of abstinence all depend on controlling sexual behavior.

Continuous abstinence means choosing not to have vaginal, anal, or oral intercourse. It is the only birth control and protection method that is 100 percent effective.

Periodic abstinence means not having sex while a woman is ovulating.

Outercourse is sex play without intercourse. It is a risky method.

Withdrawal means the male tries pulling his penis out of the female's vagina before ejaculation. Many other methods of birth control are much more effective.

Chapter 3

Abstinence and Withdrawal

Abstinence requires discipline. Sexual abstinence means avoiding intercourse. Several forms of sexual abstinence include continuous abstinence, periodic abstinence, and outercourse.

Continuous Abstinence

Continuous abstinence means that individuals or couples choose not to have intercourse. They do not engage in sex play, such as heavy petting or body rubbing, that might lead to intercourse. Teens who have been sexually active may believe they cannot be abstinent. This isn't the case. You always can choose abstinence.

The 1996 Welfare Reform Act provided nearly $440 million over 5 years for sex education programs that teach abstinence. As a result, more and more schools in the United States are promoting an abstinence-only approach to birth control.

Millie, Dom, and Marc, Age 17

Millie, Dom, and Marc are in the same class. All three have chosen abstinence but for different reasons. Millie wants to concentrate on sports and schoolwork. She thinks being sexually active would interfere with her goals. Dom knows he's not ready to have sex. He has just started dating. Marc just wants to wait until he meets someone special.

Effectiveness

Continuous abstinence is the only reversible birth control method that is 100 percent effective. Strictly speaking, it means no vaginal, oral, or anal intercourse. Thus, it is the only method that also provides 100 percent protection against STDs.

Pros and Cons

Continuous abstinence has several advantages for teens. Female teens who postpone sex until they are older can protect their health. They are less likely to damage their cervix. They also are less likely to have problems with fertility, which is the ability to have a baby. Continuous abstinence has no medical side effects and costs nothing.

Continuous abstinence can be difficult for many people, especially teens. Growth hormones that control sexual development cause strong sexual urges at this age. Another disadvantage is that people may forget to use other birth control and protection if they stop abstaining.

Periodic Abstinence

Periodic abstinence means that a male-female couple does not have sex while the woman is ovulating. There is less chance of pregnancy if the couple does not have sex while one of the ovaries is releasing an egg. Periodic abstinence also is called the rhythm method or natural family planning. Both partners need to be committed to this method for it to work.

How It Works

A woman may use one or more of the following methods to figure out her fertile time. This is the time of the month when she most likely could become pregnant.

Rhythm, or calendar, method. This method depends on a woman's having regular menstrual cycles, which many teens do not have. The usual fertile time is midway between periods, about 14 days before a female starts her period. The woman marks on a calendar the days it may be somewhat safe to have sex and the days it may be unsafe. She may need to chart her periods for 8 to 12 months before a definite pattern appears.

Basal body temperature. With this method, the woman takes her temperature every day before getting out of bed. She uses a special thermometer that measures 10ths of a degree. Slight changes in body temperature can signal an egg's release.

Effectiveness ratings indicate how well a certain birth control method protects against pregnancy. An example is an effectiveness rating of 98 percent. That means that of 100 women using the method, 2 are likely to become pregnant.

Cervical mucus. Changes in mucus, or fluid, from the cervix can indicate ovulation. Cervical mucus is discharged, or released, from the vagina. It usually looks cloudy and feels sticky. Before ovulation, cervical mucus becomes clear and slippery like egg white. There also is more of it.

Ovulation kits. Ovulation kits test the chemical balance of a woman's urine each day of the month. They cost about $35 each and can be purchased without a prescription.

Effectiveness

When used correctly, periodic abstinence is 99 percent effective in preventing pregnancy. However, many people don't use birth control and protection methods correctly. In this ordinary use, the effectiveness rate drops to 80 percent. Periodic abstinence does not protect against STDs. This complex method generally is for couples who are in a long-term, faithful relationship.

Pros and Cons

Periodic abstinence is a natural method. There is nothing to insert or put on and no pill to take. Periodic abstinence has no side effects. Its only costs are the thermometer and ovulation kits. Periodic abstinence can be used with other birth control methods.

Periodic abstinence takes a lot of work to be successful. It can be difficult to be sure if ovulation is occurring. Many couples do not like having sex only when a calendar or a thermometer tells them it's okay. Periodic abstinence usually is not recommended for teens. Teen menstrual cycles tend to be irregular. This makes it difficult to keep track of ovulation.

Outercourse

Outercourse is sexual play without intercourse. It may include kissing, hugging, holding hands, touching, and mutual masturbation, or rubbing the genitals for pleasure. It also may include petting above or below the waist, body rubbing, and kissing the genitals.

Effectiveness

Outercourse can be 100 percent effective in preventing pregnancy. However, pregnancy is possible if semen is spilled near the opening of the vagina. Outercourse can be effective against STDs. However, it does not protect against HIV or other infections if body fluids are exchanged. Also, if one person's warts or herpes contact another person's skin, infection is possible.

Pros and Cons

Outercourse can satisfy sexual urges without risking pregnancy or disease. Partners can learn more about their body and what gives them pleasure. Outercourse has no side effects or cost.

Outercourse is almost the same as foreplay. It quickly can turn into intercourse if a couple is not careful. Couples who choose outercourse should talk and set limits ahead of time. They should have another birth control or protection method ready in case they change their mind.

Withdrawal

Will begged Anna to have sex. **Will and Anna, Age 16** "Come on, Anna," he said. "Let's do it. I'll pull out in time. You won't get pregnant. I promise." Anna wasn't so sure about Will's method of birth control.

Will wants to use a form of birth control called withdrawal, which is interrupted sexual intercourse. The male tries to prevent sperm from entering the vagina by withdrawing his penis just before ejaculation.

Birth Control and Protection

Myth: You can't get pregnant the first time you have sex.

Fact: Twenty percent of first teen pregnancies happen within the first month of becoming sexually active. Fifty percent of pregnancies occur within the first six months of first intercourse.

Withdrawal should not be relied on as a form of birth control. It does not protect against STDs and is a poor method of birth control. Male teens have difficulty knowing exactly when ejaculation will occur and then withdrawing in time. They may lack control of ejaculation.

Even if the male withdraws in time, the risk of pregnancy is high. Pre-ejaculate fluid that contains sperm may escape into the vagina before ejaculation. This can cause pregnancy. If semen is spilled outside the vagina, sperm sometimes still can find their way to the uterus.

Points to Consider

Why might a teen choose to be abstinent? What is the attitude toward abstinence among your friends?

How could a girl who has never had intercourse become pregnant?

Why is discipline important to abstinence?

Many schools advocate abstinence as the only birth control and protection method for teens. Do you agree or disagree with this policy? Explain.

How might withdrawal be hard on the emotions of a couple?

Chapter Overview

Condoms and spermicides are barrier methods of birth control. Condoms prevent pregnancy by catching and holding sperm. Spermicides prevent pregnancy by killing sperm.

Next to abstinence, the male latex condom provides the best protection against STDs, including HIV. For this reason, it frequently is used with other birth control methods.

The several types of spermicides include foam, cream and gel, suppositories, and contraceptive film. Spermicides are more effective in preventing pregnancy when used with other barrier methods. Spermicides may give some protection against STDs.

Condoms and spermicides are available over-the-counter. They are inexpensive and easy to obtain and use.

Dental dams provide protection against STDs during oral sex.

Chapter 4

Condoms, Spermicides, and Dental Dams

Male Condoms

Many sexually active teens choose male condoms as their first method of birth control. Condoms are a physical barrier. They catch and hold sperm. Male condoms made from latex also prevent viruses and bacteria from passing between partners. Thus, they protect against pregnancy and STDs. Latex condoms are recommended for use with other birth control methods.

How to Put On and Take Off a Male Condom

1. Before sexual contact starts, put on the condom while the penis is erect. Pinch the condom tip to remove any air. Slowly unroll the condom over the shaft of the penis. Leave a half-inch or 1.5 centimeters at the tip to collect semen. (Some condoms have a built-in reservoir, or space for semen.)

2. Right after ejaculation, while the penis is still erect, hold onto the base of the condom. Withdraw the penis from your partner's vagina or anus. Then hold the rim of the condom and slowly withdraw the penis from the condom. Make sure no semen spills.

3. Tie the open end of the condom and throw it away. Don't flush condoms down the toilet. They can clog it.

What Male Condoms Are Like

A male condom is a sheath of thin latex rubber, polyurethane (plastic), or animal tissue. It fits snugly over the erect penis to keep semen from entering the vagina, anus, or mouth. Condoms protect the penis, vagina, cervix, anus, and mouth from STDs. However, other areas can be exposed to STDs during sexual contact. The open end of a condom has a rubber ring to keep it in place.

Condoms come rolled up in individual packages. They come in different sizes and are either dry or lubricated. Lubricated condoms ease penetration of the penis into the vagina or anus. Condoms coated with a spermicide for extra protection also are available.

How to Use Male Condoms

Condoms are used once and then thrown away. It is important to put condoms on before any genital contact. This helps prevent semen from spilling near the vagina and body fluids from exchanging. Condoms must be removed carefully after ejaculation. The top of this page gives directions for putting on and taking off a male condom.

Latex and polyurethane condoms can tear and break. Condom failures almost always are the fault of the user and not the manufacturer. Here are ways to guard against condom failure:

Store condoms in a cool place and out of direct sunlight. Condoms should not be stored in wallets or glove compartments. Heat can ruin a condom.

Check the expiration date on the condom package. A condom that has passed its expiration date may be brittle, or easily broken. Spermicide is effective for only a limited time. Condoms with spermicide expire sooner than condoms without spermicide.

Carefully open the package. Using teeth or scissors can tear the condom.

Never use petroleum jelly, baby oil, cold cream, or other oil-based lubricants on latex condoms. They might add moisture, but they could cause the rubber to break. Use a water-based lubricant such as K-Y® Jelly instead.

How to Get Male Condoms

Teens can buy condoms in drugstores and supermarkets without a prescription or an identification card. Contraceptives purchased without a prescription often are called over-the-counter birth control. Condoms usually are with other personal care products, such as tampons and vaginal sprays.

"I always have a supply of condoms on hand. That way, if my boyfriend has forgotten to buy some, we're always prepared."—LaVonne, age 17

"Matthew and I make putting on condoms part of our sex play. It makes using condoms less of a hassle."
—Jeremy, age 18

Condoms also may be available from vending machines in restrooms. They can be ordered through the mail or Internet. Some high schools and health centers give free condoms to teens.

Effectiveness

Condoms are 98 percent effective in preventing pregnancy when used correctly with every act of intercourse. In ordinary use, the effectiveness rating ranges from 88 to 97 percent. It's a good idea to use spermicide along with condoms for backup protection.

Only latex condoms protect against STDs, including HIV. The effectiveness of polyurethane condoms against STDs is thought to be the same as that of latex ones. However, researchers are not certain. Condoms made from animal tissue may be more comfortable than other condoms. However, they have pores, or openings, that germs can pass through.

Pros and Cons

Condoms are inexpensive. A box of 12 dry latex condoms costs about $6. Lubricated condoms cost more. Condoms have no side effects, except for people allergic to latex. However, such an allergy is rare. People who are allergic to latex can use polyurethane condoms instead. Male condoms are one of the only contraceptive methods where the male takes the main responsibility for birth control.

Condoms have disadvantages, too. Interrupting sex to put on a condom can be inconvenient. Some males complain that condoms decrease their physical sensitivity during intercourse. Some teens may feel embarrassed about buying condoms.

Female Condoms

The female condom, or vaginal pouch, is the newest barrier method. It is made of soft plastic or polyurethane. This loose-fitting pouch has one closed end. The open end remains outside the vagina for the penis to enter. The penis can move freely inside the condom.

Female condoms come with lubrication. The lubrication helps the condom stay in place. More lubrication can be added. A male condom is not used with a female condom.

How to Use the Female Condom

The female condom is put into the vagina shortly before intercourse. It covers the cervix to keep sperm from entering the uterus. The female condom also can be placed in the anus to provide protection during anal intercourse. The top of the next page has directions for inserting a female condom into the vagina.

Inserting and Removing a Female Condom

1. Squeeze the inner ring between your fingers and insert the condom into your vagina. Push the inner ring up until it is just behind the pubic bone. Leave about 1 inch (2.5 centimeters) of the condom outside your body.

2. Right after ejaculation, squeeze and twist the outer ring and gently pull out the condom. Toss the condom in the garbage.

Effectiveness

Female condoms are from 79 to 95 percent effective in preventing pregnancy. Their effectiveness in preventing STDs is not known. They may prove to be more effective than male condoms because they cover a wider area.

Pros and Cons

Female condoms cost about $2.50 each. They can be purchased over-the-counter. Another advantage is that they can be inserted many hours before intercourse.

The female condom can be hard to insert. The outer ring may slip into the vagina. It is important to practice inserting the condom before using it with a partner.

Spermicides

Most spermicides contain the chemical nonoxynol-9. This chemical kills sperm.

Types of Spermicides

Several types of spermicides are available. Each type is placed in the vagina shortly before intercourse. Be careful not to confuse feminine care products such as douches and vaginal sprays with spermicides. Feminine care products do not protect against STDs or pregnancy.

Foam. Foam is inserted into the vagina with an applicator. It comes in a pressurized can or container which is used to fill the applicator. Some brands come with single doses inside disposable applicators. Of all the spermicides, foam is the most effective when used alone. It is even more effective with a condom.

Creams or gels. Creams or gels come in a tube. They are meant to be applied to diaphragms and cervical caps. They also may be inserted into the vagina with an applicator.

Suppositories. Suppositories are made of a solid, waxy material and shaped like a bullet. They are inserted with the fingers into the vagina. There they melt and release spermicide. One suppository is used at a time.

Contraceptive film. Each contraceptive film is 2 inches (5.1 centimeters) square and very thin. It is placed with the fingers on or near the cervix. Like suppositories, contraceptive film melts and releases spermicide.

Effectiveness

Spermicides by themselves are not as effective as other birth control methods. They are, however, better than using nothing. Spermicides work best with other barrier methods.

Spermicides may provide some protection against certain STDs. However, more research needs to be done.

Pros and Cons

Spermicides are inexpensive, over-the-counter birth control. They are easy to apply.

Spermicides can be messy. Foam can turn to liquid and leak out of the vagina. The timing for using spermicide can be tricky. A female must insert suppositories and film 15 minutes before intercourse. If more than an hour goes by before intercourse, she must insert a fresh suppository or film. Spermicide loses its effectiveness quickly. A fresh application is needed for each act of intercourse. Some people may be allergic to an ingredient in the spermicide.

Dental Dams

Dental dams are barriers that protect against STDs during oral-vaginal or oral-anal sex. A person can lick or kiss through the dam. Dental dams are a silky, thin latex material available over-the-counter. Strong plastic kitchen wrap or a latex condom (without spermicide) that has been cut to lay flat also can be used. A new dental dam should be used every time there is oral contact with the vagina or anus. Here is how to use a dental dam:

 If using a store-bought dental dam, rinse it to remove the powdery substance. Either pat the dam dry with a lint-free towel or let it air dry.

Spread the dam over your partner's entire vaginal area or anus.

Hold the edge of the dam with your hands.

Do not flip the dam over. Use only one side.

> "My girlfriend, Amy, and I always use protection. Even the first time we were together, we used some plastic wrap. Now, we usually just cut a condom and use it as a dental dam. Sometimes for a change and some fun we use mint-flavored condoms."
>
> **Sarah, Age 17**

Points to Consider

Condoms have become an important tool in protecting people's health. Why do you think this is so?

Some people believe that passing out free condoms encourages teens to be sexually active. Do you agree or disagree? Explain.

Would you choose condoms or spermicide for birth control? Why or why not?

Chapter Overview

Diaphragms and cervical caps are barrier methods of birth control. They block sperm from entering the uterus. They do not protect against STDs.

Diaphragms and cervical caps always should be used with a spermicide.

Cervical caps are smaller than diaphragms. They are harder to insert than diaphragms but can stay in the vagina longer.

A health care professional must prescribe and fit a diaphragm or cervical cap. Diaphragms and cervical caps need to be inspected regularly for damage.

Chapter 5

Diaphragms and Cervical Caps

Diaphragms and cervical caps are worn in the vagina. They block sperm from entering the uterus by covering the cervix. They don't protect against STDs.

Diaphragms

A diaphragm is a shallow latex cup with a flexible spring rim. Its original color is white, but may turn beige or tan from exposure to air. Diaphragms come in different sizes. A doctor or nurse fits a female with a diaphragm and shows her how to insert and remove it.

"Can I walk around with my diaphragm in me?" Mina asked. "Will it fall out?"

Mina, Age 18

"No, it won't fall out," the nurse replied. "If it's inserted properly, you won't even feel it. You and your partner shouldn't feel it during sex either."

"Can I wear my diaphragm when I'm having my period?"

"No, I wouldn't recommend it. The blood needs to flow out of the uterus and into the vagina through the tiny opening in the cervix."

The nurse said that with practice Mina should need only a few seconds to insert and remove her diaphragm.

Effectiveness

A diaphragm must be used with spermicide, usually a cream or gel. Without spermicide, a diaphragm is only 82 percent effective. With spermicide, this figure rises to 94 percent. Spermicide helps keep sperm from sneaking around the diaphragm into the uterus.

Birth Control and Protection

How to Use a Diaphragm

A diaphragm can be inserted up to six hours before sex. It should stay in the vagina at least six hours after sex to protect against any remaining sperm. If the diaphragm is worn more than two hours before sex occurs, more cream or gel is needed. This can be inserted with an applicator. Also, if sex occurs more than once while the diaphragm is in, more spermicide should be inserted. A diaphragm never should be left in for more than 24 hours. An odor or infection may develop. The chart on the next page tells more about inserting and removing a diaphragm.

How to Take Care of a Diaphragm

After use, a diaphragm should be washed with warm water and mild soap. Then it should be dried thoroughly and stored in its protective case and away from heat. At least once a month, the diaphragm should be checked for small holes. One way to check is holding it up to the light. Another way is filling it with water and seeing if any drops form on the other side. A diaphragm with holes should be thrown away. A diaphragm also must be replaced if it becomes stiff or gummy or has an extreme color change.

If lubrication is used, it should be a water-based product. As with latex condoms, oil-based lubricants can damage a diaphragm.

At least once a year, a doctor or nurse should check the diaphragm to see that it still fits well. If a person loses or gains 10 pounds, she may need a different size. Women often need a bigger diaphragm after having a baby because childbirth stretches the vagina.

How to Insert and Remove a Diaphragm

Inserting

1. Place a small spoonful of spermicide in the center of the cup. Rub a little around the rim. If you wish, cover the outside of the diaphragm with spermicide. Don't overdo it, or the diaphragm will become too slippery.
2. Sit, squat, lie down with your knees raised, or stand up with one leg up on a chair or the edge of the bathtub.
3. Use the fingers of one hand to pinch the sides of the diaphragm together toward the middle. Hold the lips of the vagina apart with the other hand.
4. Slip the upper end of the diaphragm far up into the vagina, behind the cervix.
5. Push the other end of the diaphragm up in front, behind the pubic bone.
6. Check the position of the diaphragm with your finger. If you push against the rubber, you will feel the cervix. It feels like the bone at the end of your nose. The springy rim holds the diaphragm in place.

Removing

1. Hook your finger under the rim of the diaphragm.
2. Gently pull the diaphragm out. Allow it to bend.
3. Wash it off.

"You should practice using your diaphragm before you need it. That's true with any contraceptive."—Susie, age 18

Advice
From Teens

Pros and Cons

Diaphragms offer several advantages.

They provide safe and easy contraception when used correctly. Diaphragms have no side effects.

They are inexpensive compared with many other birth control methods. A diaphragm costs between $13 and $25 plus the cost of exams and spermicide. One diaphragm can be used over and over. Depending on use, a diaphragm may last for several years.

Diaphragms can be used as needed. This is an advantage if a person has sex only now and then. The person doesn't have to do something every day to keep birth control effective.

Spermicide should be put only on the inside of a cervical cap. The cap stays in place by suction. That means air is drawn out of a space to create a vacuum. Putting spermicide around the rim might affect the suction.

Diaphragms have disadvantages as well.

Spermicide makes them messy.

Diaphragms increase the risk of urinary tract infections. They can press against the urethra and irritate the bladder. Urinary tract infections often cause a burning sensation during urination. Urinary tract infections can be treated.

Some people are allergic to an ingredient in the spermicide. A few people may be allergic to latex.

Cervical Caps

A cervical cap is made of flexible latex rubber and shaped like a thimble. It is smaller than a diaphragm and fits more tightly over the cervix. A health care professional must prescribe and fit a cervical cap.

Effectiveness

When used with spermicide, cervical caps are 91 percent effective. They are less effective for women who have had a baby.

Pros and Cons

Cervical caps need less spermicide than diaphragms. Additional spermicide does not need to be added before each act of intercourse. As a result, cervical caps are less messy than diaphragms. They can be inserted for a longer time before sex and kept in for up to 48 hours. Urinary tract infections are less common with cervical caps than with diaphragms.

Cervical caps are harder to insert than diaphragms. They come in only four sizes, so not every woman can be fitted with one.

Points to Consider

Do you think diaphragms and cervical caps are good methods of birth control? Why or why not?

What advantages do diaphragms and cervical caps have compared with other barrier methods? What are their disadvantages?

Why is it a bad idea for someone to let a friend use her diaphragm?

Chapter Overview

Hormonal methods use manufactured hormones to prevent pregnancy. The drugs may be swallowed, injected, or planted under the skin.

A doctor must prescribe hormonal birth control. Usually, a teen first must have a pelvic examination.

Hormonal methods can be expensive, but they are effective and convenient.

Hormonal methods are safe for most teens. However, they can cause troublesome short-term side effects in some people.

Emergency contraception reduces the chance of an unwanted pregnancy after unprotected sex.

Chapter 6

Birth Control Pills, Shots, and Implants

Birth control pills, shots, and implants use synthetic hormones to prevent pregnancy in several ways. Most often, these methods keep the ovaries from releasing an egg. Hormonal methods also thicken cervical mucus, which makes it harder for sperm to swim through and join an egg. Some methods temporarily thicken the lining of the uterus. If fertilization should occur, the egg cannot attach to the uterus.

Hormonal methods require a prescription. First, a person must see a health care professional for a complete physical. This includes an exam of the reproductive organs, or pelvic exam. The health care worker asks about the person's medical history. These steps help to make sure the method is safe for the person.

Smoking is even more dangerous than usual if a person is taking birth control pills. Teens who smoke and take birth control pills increase their risk for heart attack, blood clots, and stroke.

Hormonal methods can be expensive. They include the cost of exams as well as drugs. A teen should find out if her doctor or clinic charges according to the patient's ability to pay.

Birth Control Pills

Birth control pills are a popular method of contraception. They also are called oral contraceptives.

How to Use Birth Control Pills

The most common type of birth control pill is the combination pill. It usually combines two female hormones—estrogen and progestin. The pill should be taken at the same time each day. This helps to keep hormone levels even. It also helps as a reminder to take it. One idea is to make the pill part of a daily routine. For example, one teen takes her pill right after brushing her teeth in the morning.

One pill pack lasts a month. Each pill in the pack has a calendar number. This helps to keep the teen on schedule. Pill packs cost between $15 and $25 each.

Effectiveness

Birth control pills prevent pregnancy almost 99 percent of the time. To be effective, however, they must be taken exactly as prescribed. Forgetting to take a pill risks possible pregnancy. A person should ask her doctor what to do if she misses a pill. A backup birth control method should be used the first month of taking the pill. This allows time for the pill to work.

Antibiotics affect the way birth control pills work. Females on birth control pills should still continue on the pill and use foam and condoms while taking antibiotics.

Pros and Cons

Birth control pills are popular because they are effective and convenient. There is nothing to put in place before sex. Birth control pills can help teens with menstrual problems have more regular and less painful periods. Many girls and women find that birth control pills help clear up their skin.

Like other drugs, birth control pills can have side effects. They can cause weight loss or gain, headaches, dizziness, depression, and nausea. Nausea is a feeling of the need to throw up. These side effects may disappear after a few months. If not, a different dose or brand might work better. Not everyone who takes the pill experiences these side effects. Some people don't have any side effects.

Depo-Provera®

Birth control also can be injected. Depo-Provera consists of the hormone progestin. It is the most common birth control injection. Young women who cannot take birth control pills with estrogen usually can take Depo-Provera.

How to Use Depo-Provera

A doctor or nurse uses a needle to inject the drug into the female's arm or buttock. This is the back of the hip that forms the fleshy part where one sits. The first shot is given during a person's period. This ensures she is not already pregnant.

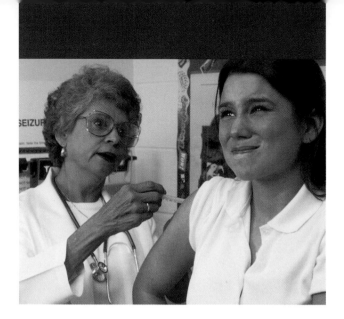

Depo-Provera protects against pregnancy for 12 weeks. After that, another shot is needed. Each shot costs between $30 and $75.

Effectiveness
Depo-Provera is close to 100 percent effective. The drug takes effect almost immediately.

Pros and Cons
Depo-Provera provides effective and long-lasting pregnancy protection. There is no daily pill to remember. It is the most private form of birth control. There is no packaging or device for others to see.

Depo-Provera can cause side effects such as weight gain, headaches, depression, and irregular, late, or missed periods. However, not everyone experiences these side effects. If pregnancy is desired, a woman must wait until the drug wears off. Some studies suggest that young women who use Depo-Provera over time may lose bone mass. Loss of bone material increases the risk of fractures, or breakage. For this reason, some people on Depo-Provera take calcium supplements, or tablets.

Norplant is the brand name for a birth control implant. This type of birth control is inserted under the skin.

How to Use Norplant

Norplant consists of six rubbery capsules. Each capsule is about 1 inch (2.5 centimeters) long and thinner than a matchstick. The capsules constantly release progestin into the bloodstream.

Elisa, Age 15

Elisa made an appointment to get Norplant. At the clinic, the doctor numbed her arm with an anesthetic. Then he made a small cut on the underside of her upper arm. He inserted the Norplant in a fan shape and put two small bandages over the area. No stitches were needed. The procedure was over in 10 minutes.

Norplant protects against pregnancy for five years. It costs between $500 and $600. After five years, the implant must be removed. A health care professional can remove the implant any time during the five years. Removal costs between $100 and $200.

Effectiveness

Norplant is nearly 100 percent effective. Protection begins 24 hours after insertion.

Pros and Cons

Except for the IUD, Norplant provides the longest-lasting birth control of any reversible method. It doesn't require checking or cleaning. There is nothing to remember, except to have it removed after five years.

Morning-after pills do not cause an abortion.
Because they are used within three days of sex,
these pills prevent pregnancy.

Norplant may cause irregular, late, or missed periods, as well as
headaches, weight gain, and nausea. The capsules may be
noticeable, especially if the teen's arm is thin or muscular. Some
studies suggest that the progestin in Norplant may lead to loss of
bone mass in young women. So some people take extra calcium.

Emergency Birth Control Pills

Emergency contraception is used after unprotected sex or an
accident with birth control, such as a condom breaking. It also
may be used following a rape, or forced sex.

Special birth control pills, known as morning-after pills, may
provide emergency contraception. These pills contain higher doses
of estrogen and progestin than regular birth control pills.
Morning-after pills usually consist of four pills in two doses. The
first two pills are taken within 72 hours of having unprotected
sex. The second two pills are taken 12 hours later.

Morning-after pills are at least 75 percent effective in preventing
pregnancy. They do not protect against infection. They will not
work if the egg and sperm have already implanted into the
uterine wall.

If you need emergency contraception, go to a doctor or family-planning clinic immediately. You can call the Emergency Contraception Hot Line 1-888-Not-2-Late (888-668-2528) for the locations of nearby clinics that can help.

Emergency contraception pills (ECPs) now are available by prescription. A person can get them ahead of time and have them on hand at home. Morning-after pills are not for regular use. Emergency contraception should not take the place of well-planned birth control.

Points to Consider

Compare hormonal methods of birth control with barrier methods. What are the advantages and disadvantages of each method?

Why should a person never let a friend borrow her birth control pills?

Why are Depo-Provera and Norplant even more effective than birth control pills?

Chapter Overview

Before becoming sexually active it is important for teens to work through some important questions. They also must be ready to guard against unplanned pregnancy and disease.

Teens who are sexually active must talk with their partner about birth control and protection.

Teens have a legal right to confidential reproductive health care.

Teens can get help with birth control from many sources. These include school nurses, family doctors, school-based health clinics, family-planning clinics, and teen hot lines.

Every teen can work toward lessening the number of unplanned pregnancies and STDs.

Chapter 7

Getting Help With Birth Control and Protection

Sex is a natural and an important part of life. Before making a decision to become sexually active, it will help to have worked through the following questions:

Do I know how pregnancy happens?

Do I understand the dangers of STDs?

Am I emotionally ready to have sex? How will I feel afterward?

Will being sexually active interfere with my goals and plans?

If you decide to become sexually active, you must guard against unplanned pregnancy and disease. This is important for both you and your partner.

Talking About Birth Control and Protection

Being involved in a sexual relationship requires communication between partners. It also requires discussion about birth control and protection. Before becoming sexually active, you may want to talk with a parent or other trusted adult. You can talk with this person about preventing pregnancy and STDs.

Daniel and Kira, Age 17

Daniel and Kira have been dating for almost a year. They feel they are mature enough to begin a sexual relationship, but they also want to be responsible. Daniel and Kira decided to talk with Daniel's brother, Miguel, about birth control. Miguel is older than Daniel and is married. Miguel was glad Daniel and Kira were taking their time and thinking through their decision. Miguel helped them make an appointment with a counselor at a family-planning clinic.

Birth Control and Protection

According to one study, more than one in three teens say they are not comfortable talking about birth control with their parents.

Talk with a potential sexual partner. Let the person know your position on birth control and protection. If you need to insist on birth control or protection, ask yourself the following question. Do I really want to have sex with this person? If you are in a committed relationship, decide together what you will do. Here are tips for talking about birth control and protection with a partner:

Practice what you will say.

Find a quiet place.

Ask for feedback.

Teens' Rights to Reproductive Health Care

Currently, all states allow teens to obtain contraceptives and treatment for STDs without their parents' permission or knowledge. Some states, however, give doctors the choice of whether to inform parents.

Should teens be allowed privacy in seeking reproductive health care? Opponents say that parents have the right to know if their children are seeking contraceptive services. They believe parents have the right to make health care decisions for their children. They also believe that confidential access to birth control encourages teens to be sexually active.

Did You Know?

Abortion is a procedure that ends a pregnancy. It is not a form of birth control. An abortion takes place after pregnancy has occurred. The idea of birth control is to prevent pregnancy in the first place.

Supporters agree that involving parents is desirable. However, they recognize that many teens may not seek birth control and protection if they have to involve parents. Supporters also believe that teens should be encouraged to take responsibility for their own health care.

Where to Go for Help With Birth Control and Protection

Teens can get help with birth control and protection from several sources. Deciding where to go may depend on four Cs.

Confidentiality. What is the policy on telling parents? If you use your family's medical insurance, will the insurance company inform your parents? These questions are important if you do not want your parents to know that you are seeking birth control or protection.

Comfort. Will you feel at ease going for help or will you feel embarrassed?

Convenience. Can you get to a source of help easily, or will transportation be a problem? Can you go at a time that fits your schedule?

Cost. Will you be able to afford the services?

Birth Control and Protection

School Nurse

You can ask your school nurse for information about birth control and protection. The nurse may be able to tell you the names and locations of clinics in your area.

Private Physician

You might see a doctor in private practice. The doctor, however, may feel obligated to tell your parents. The doctor may ask for a consent form from your parents. The fees for private physicians often are higher than fees for clinic physicians. Ask about cost and confidentiality when you call for an appointment.

School-Based Health Center

Many schools have health centers that provide reproductive health services for young people. Parents may have to sign a consent form for their child to use the health center. However, they are not told when the teen seeks service. Patient records are not available to teachers or school officials.

Family-Planning Clinic

You may have a family-planning clinic in your area. Family-planning clinics provide birth control information and give out contraceptives. Teens often can receive services at low or no cost. Look under *Clinics* or *Planned Parenthood* in the telephone book.

Teen Hot Lines

Teen hot lines are a way to find out about contraceptive methods and STDs. Staff can direct teens to helpful resources. See the *Useful Addresses and Internet Sites* section at the back of this book.

"Ever since I was little, my mom has been straightforward with me about body functions and sex. She hopes I'll wait to have sex until I'm older, but she's also realistic. Mom was the first to show me how to use a condom."—Erik, age 18

Preventing Teen Pregnancy and STDs

Here are some things you can do to help ease the problem of STDs and unplanned pregnancies:

Exercise responsibility in your own decision making. If you are sexually active, use birth control and protection. Choose the method best for you.

Make your point of view on birth control known. You may believe that abstinence is the only choice for teens. You may believe that teens should have access to contraceptives. Either way, you can work toward the goal of reducing unplanned teen pregnancies. Join an organization that supports your point of view. Write letters to lawmakers and other public officials about your concerns.

Lobby for better sex education in your school. Tell teachers and other officials that you want more information about birth control and STDs. Ask for information on forming healthy relationships and talking with parents about sex.

Support community programs that help teens. These programs encourage teens to avoid negative risk-taking behavior, including unprotected sex. They help teens to become responsible, healthy adults.

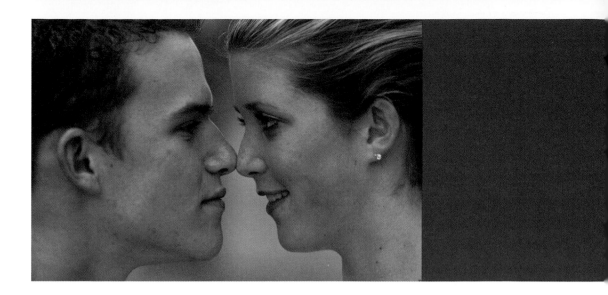

Help friends avoid risky situations. Getting drunk or high increases the chance of having unprotected sex. Encourage friends to join you in fun activities that don't include alcohol or other drugs.

Help educate other students. You may hear other teens talking about pregnancy and birth control. They may have some false ideas. Help them learn the facts.

Points to Consider

Should teens have the right to obtain birth control and protection without their parents' knowledge? Why or why not?

Parents and other adults often encourage teens to be abstinent. At the same time, they may say, "But if you do have sex, be sure to use protection." Do you think this sends a confusing message to teens? Why or why not?

What can your school do to help prevent unwanted teen pregnancies and STDs? What should parents do?

Glossary

abortion (uh-BOR-shuhn)—a medical procedure that ends a pregnancy

abstinence (AB-stuh-nenss)—choosing not to have sexual relations

condom (KON-duhm)—a barrier that fits over the penis or inside the vagina or anus

contraceptive (kon-truh-SEP-tiv)—a device such as a condom or birth control pill that prevents or reduces the risk of pregnancy

dental dam (DEN-tuhl DAM)—a flat sheet of latex used for protection against STDs during oral sex

ejaculation (ee-jak-yoo-LAY-shuhn)—the release of semen from the penis during the peak of male sexual arousal

fertilization (fur-tuh-luh-ZAY-shuhn)—the union of a male sex cell (sperm) and a female sex cell (egg)

genitals (JEN-i-tulz)—the sex organs

hormone (HOR-mohn)—a chemical in the body that controls growth, sexual development, and body functions

masturbation (mass-tur-BAY-shuhn)—rubbing or touching of the sex organs for pleasure

ovulation (ov-yuh-LAY-shuhn)—the process by which an ovary releases an egg

semen (SEE-muhn)—white, sticky fluid released from the testes that contains sperm

sexual intercourse (SEK-shoo-wuhl IN-tur-korss)—penetration of the penis into the vagina, anus, or mouth

sexually transmitted disease (STD) (SEK-shoo-wuhl-lee transs-MIT-tuhd duh-ZEEZ)—a disease that is spread through sexual contact between people

spermicide (SPURM-uh-side)—a substance that kills sperm

virus (VYE-ruhss)—a tiny organism that can cause disease

For More Information

Endersbe, Julie K. *Sexually Transmitted Diseases: How Are They Prevented?* Mankato, MN: Capstone, 2000.

Endersbe, Julie K. *Teen Sex: Risks and Consequences.* Mankato, MN: Capstone, 2000.

Knowles, John, and Marcia Ringel. *All About Birth Control.* New York: Three Rivers Press, 1998.

Peacock, Judith. *Abstinence: Postponing Sexual Involvement.* Mankato, MN: Capstone, 2001.

Useful Addresses and Internet Sites

Advocates for Youth
1025 Vermont Avenue Northwest
Suite 200
Washington, DC 20005
www.advocatesforyouth.org

Health Canada
Division of STD Prevention and Control
Bureau of HIV/AIDS and STD
Brooke Claxton Building
Tunney's Pasture, Postal Locator 0900 B1
Ottawa, ON K1A 0K9
CANADA
www.hc-sc.gc.ca

National Campaign to Prevent Teen Pregnancy
1776 Massachusetts Avenue Northwest
Suite 200
Washington, DC 20036
www.teenpregnancy.org

Planned Parenthood Federation of America
810 Seventh Avenue
New York, NY 10019
1-800-230-PLAN (800-230-7526)
www.plannedparenthood.org

Planned Parenthood Federation of Canada
1 Nicholas Street, Suite 430
Ottawa, ON K1N 7B7
CANADA
www.ppfc.ca

American Social Health Association
www.iwannaknow.org
Contains games, information, chat, and
resources on teen sexual health

Coalition for Positive Sexuality
www.positive.org
Provides facts about safer sex for teens as well
as access to experts who answer e-mail
questions about sex

drDrew.com
www.drdrew.com
Provides advice and educational articles
related to sexual issues that affect teens and
young adults

Peer Health Williams College
http://wso.williams.edu/orgs/peerh/sex/safesex
Discusses methods of contraception, includes
some illustrations, as well as a variety of safer
sex activities

CDC National STD Hot Line
1-800-227-8922

Emergency Contraception Hot Line
1-800-584-9911

Teen and AIDS Hot Line
1-800-440-TEEN (800-440-8336)

Index

Index continued